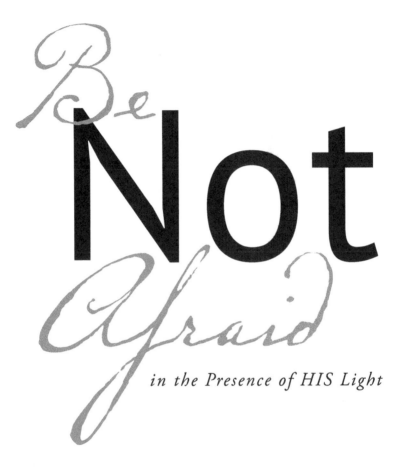

Be Not Afraid

in the Presence of HIS Light

Maureen Bishop Gilna

ISBN: 1482093332
ISBN-13: 9781482093339

Library of Congress Control Number: 2013901803
CreateSpace Independent Publishing Platform, North Charleston, SC

Dedication

I dedicate this book to:

Every person who shared in this miracle with me.

May this book
bring you comfort —
Maureen

The Promise

A young nine-year-old blonde girl watched in wonder as her class members passed little red Gideon Bibles among themselves in the schoolroom. A church group delivered the bibles throughout the grade school. She eagerly accepted this precious gift, unaware about how crucial the contents would be in her coming days.

She quickly and carefully flipped through the pages with excitement, scanning each page one at a time. Matthew, Mark, Luke, John. What a treasure to behold. As she finished her scanning, she came to the very last page of the book. The page began with the title, "Have you given your life to Christ?" Since she was only nine years old and she had not had any religious training in any church, she could not remember ever having given her life to Christ. On the last page, there was a place to write her name and date. She quickly did so, not even reading the full content of the promise that followed. She just signed it because it looked important to see her name in print on that page.

She saved this little red book and she still has it today, tucked away among the treasures of her past. It still reads: I, Maureen Bishop, hereby give my life to Christ and promise to follow His teachings throughout my life. She has taken the book out many times to read it. As the years have gone by, she has realized what this promise means. It was the beginning of a very special life—a life in the presence of His Light.

Prelude

The year was 1972.

My husband, Richard, and I had been married for fourteen years. We had four beautiful children. Michele was eleven years old, Cheryl was ten, Michael was eight, and Christine was seven. Our firstborn had been born prematurely, living for only fifteen hours. Her name was Mary Theresea.

We owned and operated a Registered Holstein farm in Corunna, Michigan. We worked very hard as a family to maintain it. This meant that most of our time was dedicated to producing milk, and raising cows and calves. We also worked the fields to provide food for our livestock. We were involved in our community and our family volunteered when we needed to. The children were active in school. We belonged to St. Paul Catholic Church in Owosso, Michigan. I volunteered there as a religious education teacher. It was a good time in our lives and we were very happy.

It was also the time when this miraculous story begins.

Springtime Miracle

Springtime is the second busiest time of the year for a farmer.

Spring is also a time for personal reflection and renewal. It is a time for decisions in our spiritual lives—a season that brings God's gifts of forgiveness and hope, and the miracles of life, death, and resurrection.

I am going to share with you how God has worked in my life and how He has shown me our purpose on earth. I will show you how He touched others through my suffering and how He used me for His purpose. This story involves many beautiful people in my family, community and church.

What I am sharing with you is my own special experience.

I am in no way trying to sway your personal and spiritual beliefs.

Fall of 1972

It was the fall of 1972. I was thirty-four years old. This would be the year that I would be forever changed in both spirit and body. Five pregnancies in six years had taken their toll on my body. I began to experience physical problems and my physicians decided that I would need a hysterectomy. Since we had four beautiful children, I knew that we could be satisfied with these four special gifts from God. Still, the word *hysterectomy* stirred a sad feeling in my heart. I guess no woman ever wants to hear this word. I decided to have the surgery in late fall.

In the early 1960's, there was a renewal in the Catholic Church. This was the beginning of bringing the Catholic Church together with other established denominations throughout the world.

Around 1965, the Charismatic movement had just begun in the Catholic Church. The word *charismatic*, in this instance, meant gifts and grace from the Holy Spirit, such as healings, miracles, praying, and singing in tongues. Something special drew me to the charismatic prayer groups that were being formed throughout the nation. I was eager to learn more, and I was invited to attend a group from our church. The meeting was held at my friend Florence's home. There were about ten people who congregated there that night in October. We commenced with singing and praying. Then there was a special time for sharing. The leader of the group asked me if I had given my life to the Lord. I remember thinking to myself that I had gone through five pregnancies, been married to a dairy farmer—where hard work was essential for success—attended church regularly, and volunteered as a CCD teacher. I had been involved in my community, helping out when and where I was needed, and I felt that I had more than given my life to Christ. I viewed my life as a sacrifice. I began to rethink the answer to the question of having given my life to the Lord, in a charismatic way.

Then I remembered how I had given my life to Christ back when I was nine years old. I was a student in grade school in 1947. A church group had distributed a small red Gideon Bible to all the students in my school. I treasured my little bible and I read it faithfully. I promised to give my life to Christ on the last page of that bible. At the time, I didn't fully understand what it meant to give my life to Christ. I have kept that book all of these years. I treasure it more now than ever.

My attention came back to my thoughts about giving my life to the Lord. I decided to take this pledge again. As I sat in a chair in my friend's living room, my prayer group friends surrounded me, laying their hands on my head in prayer. I felt so relaxed and peaceful as the warmth of His Holy Spirit enveloped me. As I gazed out of the living room window into the dark black fall night, the stars were twinkling brilliantly. I felt the tremendous strength of God's love. I asked the Lord what He wanted me to do in this world for Him, and I pledged my life to accomplish that goal. This question would gnaw at me in the months to come.

As I drove home that night along the dark country road, I looked again at the pitch-dark sky and observed how brilliant the stars looked, sparkling as never before. I began to sing "Jesus I Love You" repeatedly. My love for my Lord was so strong at that moment and my heart was so happy as I continued singing. Soon, I noticed that I was singing the words in another language. The words just rolled off of my tongue as I continued to praise God. I continued to sing these words and I could not stop pouring out my heart. By the time I turned into the driveway, I felt cleansed and serene to the very core of my being.

I found out later the next day that I had experienced the gift of tongues. It is a special gift from the Holy Spirit that allows us to praise God in a different way. Thank you Lord for this gift. I learned that there are many gifts of the spirit that we are blessed with as we pray. These gifts bring our hearts and minds so very close to our Lord, leaving us in wonder and praise. Whenever my words are insufficient, my gifts reveal the deep love in my heart to my Lord.

I decided to have the hysterectomy in November. The crops would hopefully be mostly harvested and the workload would not be so heavy for my husband, Dick. My surgery was scheduled for right after Thanksgiving. Plans were made for my mother Frances and Dick's mother Catherine to take care of the children. I was so blessed to have them helping us out for a couple of weeks. I would have to be in the hospital for one week and then recuperate at home for another week. I would indeed need this help.

The surgery went well and I was soon home. In the weeks that followed, my body was healing. However, I was not feeling well at all. I was feeling terribly tired all of the time. Doctors told me that it would take a while for me to regain my strength. They told me to be patient.

After the holidays, I thought that I would be able to rest. January came and passed, and I felt no better. Again I visited the doctor. I felt that it was not normal to feel this way, and I asked for more tests. He assured me that I had experienced a hysterectomy, which was a predictably intense operation after all, and it would take time to heal. I trusted his advice. February passed very slowly; there was no change in my condition. I was so tired. I had to rest more and more after any activity. This was not like me. We attended a camper show one weekend. We had planned to purchase a camper so that we could attend the local and state Holstein shows and perhaps find a week in the summer to take a vacation. As we surveyed each camper, I found it necessary to sit down and rest at every camper we inspected. I was thinking to myself, "Enough is enough." It was then that I just knew that something was very wrong.

I decided to go to another doctor. He examined me, but he could find nothing wrong. He remarked, "After all, you must remember that you have had a hysterectomy." He then prescribed pills to help me lose weight and medication for my nerves, and he sent me on my not-so-merry way.

The pills didn't work. I then decided to make one more appointment with yet another doctor. He thought that my problem might be mental, so he suggested that I see a psychiatrist.

I returned home in despair. "Lord," I asked, "what do you want me to do?" I became very depressed and very sick. I began to give up. I had written in my diary, "Something bad is going to happen to me, but it will be good." I had no idea where this entry came from and what it meant. I decided to wait and see what God had in store for me.

The next months and weeks are hard for me to remember. I do know that I tried very hard to be active, and it took all of my strength to be a mother and wife. I did a lot of praying and trusted in God's plan for my life—or end of life.

Mother's Day

I don't remember Mother's Day very well. In the previous weeks, I had become increasingly weaker. I do remember going to school functions and leaving early because I felt extremely sick and could not sit for long. As I recall, in the days leading up to Mother's Day, I had been vomiting and I had severe diarrhea. My husband finally decided that it was time to take me to the hospital for help. From that moment on, I don't remember anything. I have to rely on the recollections of my family and friends.

I was taken to our local hospital, where my condition was labeled as colitis, which is an inflammation of the colon. I was taken to a regular room and the treatments began. The corn-planting was in full swing, and I insisted that Dick return home to tend to the farm. I assured him that I would be okay. He told me that he would see me the next day before he went out to work in the fields. He left reluctantly.

I was given intravenous solutions because my body was becoming dehydrated due to the great loss of fluids. I became much worse through the night. The next morning, the doctors diagnosed me with kidney failure. Dick was summoned to the hospital immediately. When he arrived, the doctors informed him that my kidneys were not functioning and I was declining. He was told that I needed to remain in a hospital, where dialysis was available. At that time, the only two hospitals with dialysis were in Ann Arbor and the Hurley Hospital in Flint. The doctors said that the two-hour trip to Ann Arbor would take too long and I needed immediate attention. I was taken by ambulance to Hurley, which was only about thirty minutes away.

My good friend Pat had just called our house that morning to find out how I was doing, and my mother had informed her that I was in grave health and I was being transferred to Hurley. Pat notified the prayer group immediately. The prayers went out into the community, and soon people were praying for me statewide. Many churches in the area of Owosso were notified, and they began a prayer vigil for my family and me. The prayers continued throughout the many weeks of my illness.

Diagnosis and Treatment

Upon arriving at the Flint hospital, I was put in intensive care. My body temperature reached 105 degrees and remained there for many days. Dialysis is a procedure that performs the normal duty of the kidneys and filters waste products from the blood. I was put on a peritoneal dialysis at first, which meant that the procedure was done through my abdomen. I began to convulse because of my high fever and my severe dehydration. Poisons caused by the kidney failure were ravaging my body. I soon went into a deep coma. I then was put on a regular dialysis. My condition continued to worsen as the hours went by. The nephrologists were not sure what was wrong, and they had a difficult time making a diagnosis. All efforts were being made to keep me alive.

After several days, the hospital's pediatric nephrologist diagnosed my condition after he discovered it in a pediatric journal. It was called Microangiopathic hemolytic anemia. With this condition, the blood cells flatten and become tiny blot clots. The blood clots were clogging my kidneys, causing them to shut down. In consulting other cases on record, the doctors discovered that at that time this condition was only found in children and it was fatal.

They decided to give me blood thinners to dissolve the blood clots. Unknown to anyone, I had a stomach ulcer and the blood thinners caused my stomach to hemorrhage. I was then given many units of blood.

I had the best team of nephrologists available for my care. One of the doctors was a specialist in pediatric nephrology. He was a very attentive and spiritual man. My team of nurses was very professional, and they were supportive and compassionate toward my family.

My husband, sister, brother-in law, and parents camped out in the hospital parking lot in a motor home. The hospital graciously gave them permission to stay there. They were in constant vigil. I can only guess how they must have felt at that time. They were very strong and they had great faith.

Day after day, there was no positive change in my condition. I could no longer breathe on my own and I was put on a ventilator. I was literally being kept alive by machines. My body rejected any medicine that they administered to me. I had constant convulsions. Any time any-body touched my body, or even my bed, I went into convulsions. The neurosurgeon ran tests on my brain activity. He reported to the family that my brain was deteriorating because of the trauma and fever that my body had been experiencing. He suggested that if I did live, I would be a vegetable for the rest of my life—a devastating report for my family for sure. They advised Dick to return home and prepare our four young children for my death. There was nothing that they could do for me. My body was in severe crisis. I was told later that they had not told my children the news at this time.

While all of this was going on, nephrologists from all over the United States were visiting Hurley Hospital for a convention. My family was asked if it would be all right for these doctors to examine my case and offer their opinions about what more could be done for me. Of course my family agreed. After all the doctors had examined me and reviewed my tests and records, they all agreed that everything that could be done for me was already in progress. They could offer no further advice about treatment or help. How amazing that was! What a coincidence it was that they had congregated at Hurley at the exact time I was so critical. This certainly helped my family know that I was in good and capable hands. It saved my family from feeling guilty for not being able to take me elsewhere for further diagnosis and treatment. One could only believe that God had a hand in bringing those doctors there at that specific time.

The nursing staff consisted of two very special nurses who were veterans, so to speak, of the renal unit. One of them talked with members of my family and suggested that I be taken off life support. They found it unfortunate for me to go through all of this trauma and suffering. My family refused to talk of such a thing. One family member who was very adamant about this was my mother. She refused for anyone to say, "*If* she wakes up…" She instructed them instead to say, "*When* she wakes up…"

One nurse in particular was able to work with me unlike any of the others. She encouraged my family to keep talking to me, even though I was in a deep coma. She related to them that the sense of hearing is very strong, even when the body is in crisis. At one point, a family member was present with this nurse at my side when my blood pressure began to drop drastically. This was a sign that my body was giving up. This special nurse began to yell at me to not give up. She emphasized that I had no business leaving a husband and four lovely children and that they needed me. I was told it was at that moment that my pressure began to climb. This certainly was an example of how powerful words are to those who are on the verge of dying.

My family related various stories to me about how multiple staff members were doubtful that I would recover. Days turned into weeks and there was little hope that I would recover. They observed the doctors exhausting every avenue of cure without success. Their advice was to remove me from life support and let me go peacefully.

Blessings and Friends

Every day is a busy day on a farm, especially when there are animals to take care of. Our cows had to be milked twice a day. The cows, heifers, and calves needed to be fed. Extra attention would be given to animals that had become ill. In the springtime, farm families thought of nothing but preparing the fields to plant the crops and harvest the hay.

Most of the time, the farmer's wife is a partner in operating the farm. Meals had to be prepared for the family and for the hired farm help. A large breakfast was necessary to fuel energy for the workday ahead. A midday lunch was eaten either in the field or in the house. Evening dinner came after the barn chores in the early evening had been finished. The laundry of a large farm family was never-ending. Whether it was with the house chores or the barn chores, all family members helped out to keep the operation of a farm home working smoothly.

Dick and I were very involved in our community and farm organizations. Leisure time was scarce but we managed to find some once in a while. We hired a young man who was very dedicated to his job on the farm and who was an excellent worker. We were so blessed to have him helping out at this time.

How difficult it must have been for my husband, Dick, throughout my illness. As he later explained to me, it was difficult for him to remember all that was going on. He worried constantly about the children, the farm, and me. His greatest fear was that I might not recover and that I would die. How would the children handle such a grave situation? Who would take care of them while he was at the hospital? He remarked to friends after my recovery that whenever one of our cattle needed critical medical attention, he would call the veterinarian to come to the farm and treat the animal. When a tractor or piece of machinery would break down in the field, he would call the farm equipment dealer to come fix what needed to be fixed. When I was in critical condition and dying, the only person he could call on to help was God.

Most of the fields were already plowed and prepared for spring planting before I became ill. Several good neighbors helped prepare the fields for corn planting. A good friend, Bill, brought his planting equipment to our farm and planted eighty acres of corn for us in Dick's absence. Thanks be to God for good friends.

I was told that Dick was constantly by my side. I was his first priority. His mind felt numb and he was just able to go through the motions of living. My sister, my brother-in-law, and my parents were present with him at the hospital. At home, our wonderful and faithful friends rallied around the family, generously providing help in the form of childcare, housework, food preparation, and anything else that needed to be done. Our children were attending grade school at the time. Our special neighbors moved into the neighborhood just a few months before I became ill. Their children were around the same age as our children. These neighbors graciously opened their homes to our children when necessary. Another neighbor had a beautiful pool and welcomed the children to her home often. Our children were well taken care of.

At one special time, our community of friends from several farm organizations, prayer groups, and churches prepared a special prayer service on my behalf. This was held at St. Paul's Church, where we were members. I was told that it was a beautiful service and well attended. What a beautiful gift to my family that service was.

In the Presence of His Light

Meanwhile, when all of this was going on in my body, my spirit was in a world of its own. The loud ringing sensation in my head was very noisy and annoying. The noise disturbed me immensely. I felt no pain but I did feel uncomfortable and uneasy.

I found myself walking slowly down a very long hallway. It seemed to be in a large building that had many rooms on each side of the hall. It reminded me of a hospital hallway. I had the feeling that someone was following me. I turned around to investigate who this might be. There, a short distance behind me, was a group of about ten people who I did not recognize. They had no faces. I felt very uneasy about their presence, and I turned and walked swiftly away from them. I hurried my pace and as I turned around again, they were still there. I walked into the stairwell and proceeded down the steps. I opened the door to the next hall and entered it. As I continued down that hall, many other people passed by me. They did have faces, so I felt that I could reach out and ask them for help. As I did so, they acted like they did not even see me, walking right by without recognizing me. I remember one particular young person who was dressed in a white nurse's uniform and had red hair. I wasn't afraid of these people, but I was very puzzled by their behavior toward me.

I came to another stairwell. Glancing back, I could see that the faceless group was still pursuing me. They were not running but they kept up the same slow steady pace. I really wanted to get away from them but they were so hard to shake off. I walked through many halls and climbed many steps until I became so unbearably tired. I was exhausted but not afraid. I finally turned around to face them. I asked them what it was they wanted from me. I could sense that they were evil, but they did not intimidate me. I was more annoyed than anything else. I asked again what they wanted from me. They answered me in a persuasive voice: "Come with us. Come with us." I told them that I would sit down and talk with them about it, hoping that they would leave me alone. I asked them to give me just one hour of their time. To my great disappointment, they agreed. Unknown to me, I was about to experience a very important test of spiritual strength.

Suddenly, we were in a large room with a large, round wooden table. All of the faceless people who were pursuing me were seated in chairs around the table, and all of their attention was on me. They said nothing. As I gazed at their faceless bodies, I sensed their evilness even more. I wasn't frightened but the feeling was a very dark one. Finally, one of them said, "Come with us and you will be very happy and free." The unemotional and insincere tone of the voice lacked any sense of security and comfort.

At this point, as exhausted as I was, I felt very strong and positive in my spirit and faith. I knew for sure that I did not want to go with them. Because of their negative behavior, I just wanted them to leave me alone. I proceeded to inform them that it was useless for them to persuade me to go with them. My words to them began spilling from my heart at a fast rate about my love for God and my Lord and Savior.

I let them know how strong my faith was. As exhausted as I was, I felt the strength to repeatedly emphasize my love for the Lord. I told them that I just wanted to be with my God and that was exactly what I was going to do. They just sat there quietly, not saying a word. There was a great silence in that big room. It lasted a while, yet I did not have anything further to say. I stood my ground in silence. Finally one of the figures stood up. Then the next one got up, and one by one the rest followed suit until they were all standing. Then one by one, without saying anything, they exited, leaving me alone in the room. I felt a great sense of relief and a tremendous sense of joy.

Suddenly, I was thrust into a very bright light. It was blinding but it did not feel uncomfortable. It felt like someone was holding me in a warm and loving embrace. The intense ringing in my head had disappeared. It was very quiet and relaxing. I had the sense of weight-lessness. It was as if I were comfortably floating on air. I felt so cool, comfortable, and fresh. The bright light was intense, and it continued cradling me in love. I knew that I was in a very special place. I have never been on a mountain peak, but that was what I likened it to. I remember remarking out loud, "So this is what it is like to die!"

The light continued to envelope me as I continued in a euphoric suspension. I had no thoughts of the past or the future. I just knew that I very much enjoyed being where I was. I felt my mind clearing. I also felt like I was being spoken to in a very special way. There were no words like those we hear from others. It is difficult to describe. My mind was being filled with information, and I seemed to understand it. I wanted so badly to stay where I was at that point, surrounded by God's Divine Love. However, I was informed that I was to return to the world, as He had work that He wanted me to do for Him.

When I understood that I had work to do for the Lord, I wondered what exactly this work would be. The answer was very simple. I was told to serve Him and that He would open the doors for me to fulfill His work.

As I continued to be blessed in the light, I felt wonderfully warm with love as I was continually fed much knowledge about life. I would realize this knowledge more fully when I returned to the world, where I would begin to serve Him.

During what seemed like an eternity of bathing in His holy light of love and knowledge, I began to notice the color green appearing around my feet. It became increasingly green until it surrounded my whole being and I was completely engulfed with it. Later on, theologians would inform me that the color green often signifies resurrection.

I have no other memory of this special place. From this heavenly experience, I have learned that even in death we might be tempted. I believe that if one is strong in faith, they will be able to overcome the temptation that Satan puts in our paths. I feel that we must pray for those who are dying to be strong. We must pray for God to protect them in their journey to His Heavenly Kingdom.

I have met many people who have had near death experiences. All of their stories are different, but most of these people received similar messages.

Prayers and More Prayers

God plants certain angels in our lives, and I myself have had many of them. My angel friend Pat, a member of my church parish, was instrumental in introducing me to the charismatic prayer group in the fall before my near death experience. Little did she know that the Lord was going to use her in my life.

Pat had become the connection between our family and the prayer community. In the spring, there was to be a Midwest Charismatic Conference at Notre Dame University in Indiana. Prayer groups from all over the Midwest would be gathering there for prayers and praise. My good friend Pat had planned on attending the conference, but she felt that she should stay home and assist my family. Our family members encouraged her to attend so that she could ask for special prayers for my recovery. Private healing prayer sessions, conducted by several experienced Catholic priests from all areas of the United States, were offered at the conference.

Pat made the decision to attend. She drove to Detroit, where she planned to ride to the conference with several Carmelite Sisters who were her friends. The Carmelite Sisters were a special order of nuns in the Catholic Church. They resided at Carmel Hall in Detroit, which was a large residence for assisting the frail, the ill, and senior citizens from the area.

According to my friend, the conference was well attended. She had made plans to attend a healing prayer time especially for me. However, the conference was coming to a close, and she could not attend a healing session because of the long line of people who were ahead of her requesting prayers. Her heart was very heavy and she had to leave the conference in great disappointment.

As she was traveling back home with the sisters, she expressed her disappointment at not accomplishing her mission. They assured her that she still had a chance to attend a healing session with a priest from New Jersey, who would be staying at Carmel Hall that evening. He was scheduled to catch a flight from Detroit to his home the next day. They would ask him to pray with my friend the next morning before he left.

The next morning, the priest, several Carmelite Sisters, and my friend Pat met for a special hour of prayer for me. She relates that as they were praying, the priest stopped and became silent for a long moment. As he resumed the prayer, he remarked that he was led to pray for something special. He then began again by asking for a special prayer of forgiveness for everyone who needed to be forgiven in my family. Unknown to those present, this was indeed a special prayer that had great significance for me. Praise God for that prayer session. Prayers concluded and my friend thanked the priest. She then continued her journey back to Owosso.

Upon returning home, she promptly called my mother to relate her experience at the prayer session and to find out how I was doing. My mother answered the phone. Hearing my friend's voice, she began to cry. My friend later told me that she thought that I had died. She began to tell my sobbing mother that she was so sorry. My mother replied, "Oh no, you don't understand! This morning, Maureen opened her eyes and spoke for the first time. She is out of her deep coma!" They both continued to cry in joy and thanksgiving.

The Love of a Brother

My youngest brother, Fred, was with me as much as he could be. He had a great sense of humor and one never knew—or knows to this day—what kind of prank or smart remark he might make. I was still in a coma. It was his desire to sit with me while I was undergoing dialysis treatment. These treatments were administered to me every other day. The blood in my body was drawn into a special machine to be cleaned. It was then returned to my body, free of particles that would harm me. Fred would persuade the attending nurse to let him sit by my side during this treatment.

My lips had been cut and they were swollen as a result of my continuous convulsions. My teeth would gnash and grind, severely injuring my lips. Fred would gently put very small pieces of ice on my lips and mouth area. As he did so, he would talk to me. I was in a deep coma, and was unaware of anything that was going on. He kept on with the conversation anyway. He would inform me about what activities were going on at home, what the weather was like, or any other bits of news that he could think of.

One particular day, as he was about to place some cool ice chips on my lips, my brother asked me if I would like some more. I opened my eyes for the first time and emphatically said, "No." My sister said he came bolting out of the room with great excitement, eager to tell the staff about what just happened. This was my first step toward returning to the world.

The Golden Chalice

It was like waking up from a long and meaningful sleep. I was not in pain, but I was extremely weak and tired. I was trying to remember what had just happened to me. I remembered the light. The place filled with a warm and wonderful feeling. It was as if Jesus our Lord were right there with me in my room. I began talking to Him as if He were standing next to me. I felt knowledgeable about so many things. For instance, I was assured that I was going to be all right and that others would be questioning how well my mind would be. I was very careful when the doctors and the staff asked me questions. The medical staff informed me that I had been through a very serious time, and as a result I would need dialysis for the rest of my life because my kidneys were not functioning. Immediately, I told them that they were wrong. I related that somebody in the light had let me know that I was going to be okay and that I would recover completely and have good health again. The nurses and doctors looked at me sympathetically, but they never said a word. I felt so strongly in my heart that I was right.

After being in the intensive care room for over three weeks, I was finally taken to a regular hospital room. The doctors felt that I was out of immediate danger, but I still had to be watched very carefully for any possible decline. As I drifted in and out of sleep, I observed the room that I was in. I noticed that the window view was not very good. It gave me a view of one of the hospital's brick walls. All in all, despite the view, the room was very warm, comfortable, and peaceful.

My sister Janis, who was—and still is—an accomplished artist, created a beautiful painting for my wall. As she explained later, she worked on this creation over the many days of my illness. The painting hung on the wall just to the right of bed, so it was visible to me at all times. It brought me much comfort. The chalice was painted gold and the background of the painting had beautiful shades of royal purple and deep red. My eyelids felt very heavy and I opened them very little. When I did open them for a few minutes at a time, I focused on the picture of the chalice.

I could also feel the warm and soothing presence of someone constantly standing at the foot of my bed. My eyes were still not focusing very well, and I just wanted to sleep. Whoever was standing there brought me much peace and relaxation. I felt no fear or pain.

One day, the nurse who attended me was giving me a bed bath and trying to involve me in a conversation. "Don't you ever feel alone in this room by yourself?" she asked me. The question was very puzzling to me. "I am not alone. Someone is always standing at the foot of my bed." I answered. I noticed that the look on her face was one of surprise, but she could not disagree with me, so she did not challenge my answer at that time. She had probably been told to be patient with my comments. After all, my mind might not be completely normal ever again.

As the hours turned into days and I began to focus more clearly, the image of the person at the foot of my bed seemed to drift slowly toward the picture of the chalice on the wall. The person and the chalice seemed to blend together, continuing to bring me warm feelings of peace. It remained there for many days. As I began to fully recover, I no longer felt the presence of this person. The warmth and the peace it held for me now resided in the chalice itself. I truly believed that person at the foot of my bed was my guardian angel, who had been sent to watch over and protect me.

I began to feel much better every day, and I quickly became more alert and full of life.

The day came for me to take my first steps. Several nurses carefully assisted me out of bed. A doctor was also present. I was doing very well until they asked me to step on the scales to be weighed. It was at that point that I lost consciousness. When I came to, I was back in my bed. I was informed that I had fainted. I replied that the last thing I remembered was looking down at the scales. I joked that I had seen that I had lost almost thirty pounds, and I had fainted from shock. We all had a good laugh. At least my sense of humor had not been lost.

Children's First Visit

It was a very long time before I was allowed to see my children. When Dick came to visit me, he would bring back stories of their activities. One particular story was about the children riding their bikes down to the creek to play in the mud. I became very alarmed. Because of my grave condition, I had slight amnesia. I thought that the children were still riding their tricycles. I was crying and insisting that they were far too young to be traveling down the road by themselves. At that point, Dick decided that I needed to see the children.

I will always remember waiting for that special day. Those four precious faces were a sight for me to behold. It took a few minutes for them to feel comfortable because they had not seen me for four weeks. They didn't quite know what to say. My daughter Cheryl, who remembers the event, says that I commented on her new shoes and how lovely they were. She remembers thinking of how odd that remark was because I was the one who had bought them for her. Everything looked so new to me. Before long the four of them were bubbling over with stories and news from home.

The children also recalled the many pieces of children's artwork that were displayed on my hospital room walls. They had drawn some of the pictures for me. Other pictures were "get well" greetings from the third-grade religious education class that I had been teaching at the time.

The hospital gave me permission to leave the hospital for a very short time—an hour. I was allowed to take a short ride with Dick and the children. I imagine that this was allowed so that I could regain some of my memory. We only went a short way, to an ice cream shop. We ordered luscious chocolate milk shakes and enjoyed just being together once again. We returned shortly to the hospital. It was difficult for me to say goodbye to my precious children. That truly was a memorable time for all of us. Whenever I drive by this same ice cream place today, it always brings back sweet memories.

The children remark today how kind everyone who took care of them was. They also tell me how grateful they are now that they had been protected from the knowledge of how grave my condition had been.

God Willing

I can only imagine what agony my parents must have experienced as they watched over me those many days and weeks. I would like to now share with you the strong faith that my mother had throughout my ordeal.

My mother, Frances, came from a very strong German background. She was a woman of great faith in God, and she tended to look on the positive side of problems. When the doctors told my family that there was no hope for me to live, and when they suggested removing me from life support, my mother was strong in saying, "No." With a firm tone, she made sure that they understood this.

My mother's family has been in the possession of a relic of St. Catherine Labouré for many years. A relic is a part of a deceased holy person's body or belongings kept as an object of reverence. St. Catherine was born in 1806 in France. She was the ninth in a family of eleven children. Her mother died when she was nine years old. Catherine entered the Community of the Daughters of Charity of St. Vincent DePaul in Paris. There, during the first months of novitiate, she was favored with a number of Apparitions of the Blessed Virgin, who showed her the Miraculous Medal, commissioned her to have the medal made and to spread devotion to this medal. There is more to her story, but this gives you an idea how her sainthood began.

The relic is housed in a beautifully simple locket and is used to pray over a person in the family who was gravely ill. My mother had possession of the relic.

As my mother told me, she was praying constantly for me. She was at my bedside whenever she could be. There were so many times she could not be with me because of the severity of my condition. One day, she had the chance to be with me without anyone else in the room. She had brought the relic with her. This was her chance to ask St. Catherine for a special healing for me. I was still unresponsive. She placed the relic on my forehead. As she held it there for a matter of minutes, she prayed: "God, willing, please heal Maureen." As she was finished and still holding the relic in place, she related that a great surge of energy traveled up her arm and into her body. It caused her to almost lose her balance and fall to the floor. Her knees were very weak, and she could hardly hold herself up. She thought that something was wrong with her. She released the relic, left my bedside, and sat in the chair for a long time.

She did not share this story with me until about a year after I had returned home. She did not tell anyone about this experience, holding it close to her as a private moment that could not be explained to just anyone.

Sometime after she shared this story with me, I invited my mother to attend a prayer group meeting that was being held at our church. The guest speaker's subject was "The Healing Power of Touch." She sat beside me as the group watched a very special film on how healing energy is transferred from one person to another through the power of touch and prayer. When the film concluded, my mother grabbed my hand. I looked at her and there were tears in her eyes.

"That is what I experienced," she whispered emphatically. "I felt the energy. It was so strong." Together, we both realized the power of a mother's prayer. I was so grateful that she had the insight to use this powerful prayer over her daughter, who was dying.

Shortly after my mother returned home, she had written a poem entitled "God Willing."

Mother is now in her heavenly home. I still ask her for favors and prayers, and she always comes through for me. Our love is even stronger now than ever.

Dear God Willing

By Frances Bishop

Dear God willing, I softly prayed

As my hand on her young body I laid.

A beautiful mother of four

Racked with pain at death's door.

It seemed such a short time ago.

He gave her to us, to watch her grow

Into a happy girl, full of love.

Now, in my hour of need of help from you,

Show me what you would have me do.

My heart aches to see her in pain,

But surely there must be sunshine after rain.

Dear God willing was what I prayed

And hoped I would not be afraid.

If in His wisdom He should deem

To take her from this earthly scene.

Dear God willing rings in my mind

With a clear tone, one of a kind.

So I'll trust in what He is saying.

In my heart, I know He hears me praying.

The days were sad, the nights so long,

I thought we'd never sing another song.

Little did we know what was in store

For our beautiful mother of four.

Then came the day I felt God so near,

As the doctor brought us good cheer.

That beautiful mother of four

Was no longer at death's door.

Now all of our hearts were lightened,

Lives of a family brightened.

Dear God willing had been my constant plea.

Today He answered, "You trusted in me!"

My Father

My dear father Frank was a man of few words and emotions. Rarely did I see him cry. I do remember seeing him cry on the day that I got married. He was very secretive about this, though, and he probably thought I that I had not seen him—but I did. My dad, the man I worshipped throughout my life. He was a hard worker and he was dedicated to his job as a Conservation Officer. He also had other odd jobs to bring in money for the family. He never had any words of wisdom for me in life that I can remember. He rarely got very upset with me—not even when I lost the keys to the car when I was downtown at the pharmacy. He made the trip to the store to bring me another key. He had a stern look on his face, but I caught a slight smile as he turned away.

Dad was an accomplished gardener. When I married a farmer, he was thrilled. This meant that perhaps he would get a garden of his own to work in. We provided him a large area in the back of the farmhouse. After Dick carefully plowed and fertilized the future garden, it was ready to be planted. I was very grateful that Dad volunteered for and undertook this crop-growing project. The garden would not only provide food for our family; it would be a blessing for Dad. Whenever Dad had problems, he would work tirelessly in that garden. It was like a therapy for him. After he had accomplished his weeding, he would sit on his red bench at the end of the garden and look over his small plot of land. Not one weed would dare grow there. He would see it immediately and proceed to destroy it. He seemed to derive some pleasure in doing this, releasing negative energy as he destroyed those blamed weeds.

I was told that Dad cried a lot when I was dying. As a father, he could no longer make things better for me. He was there for me as much as he could be. I don't know all that went on in his head because he never shared it with me.

We have a small island in our circle driveway. On this island, my father planted a beautiful flower garden. In this flowerbed was a statue of Our Blessed Mary. Dad made sure that no weed dared grow in that flowerbed. During the time when I was dying, I was told that Dad was out there pulling those weeds out of the ground just as he had in the garden. He also planted new flower plants and cared for those flowers with much patience and love. I can only imagine the conversations that he might have had with God—and perhaps with Mary—while he was caring for that beautiful island.

Unexpected Turn of Events

I was still receiving my dialysis treatments every other day. One particular day, after receiving my treatment, a nurse was helping me into bed and straightening out my sheets to make me more comfortable. As she was doing this, I discovered a very large lump under my right upper arm. This was the arm that held the shunt that was needed for the connection to the dialysis machine. I brought this discovery to the attention of the nurse. She became very alarmed and upset, and she summoned the doctor to the room. After examination, it was determined that I had a very large blot clot that could prove to be life-threatening. I could tell that the whole staff was very concerned as they left my room. A couple of hours later, they informed me that this clot would certainly prevent them from administering the next dialysis treatment, as the clot would certainly move and cause a large problem. If I didn't have dialysis, my body would be in grave crisis once more. If the clot were left in, it might travel and cause a stroke or death. Blood thinners would be considered if it were not for the fact that I had almost bled to death weeks before with the stomach ulcer condition. I remember being so calm and positive about the whole problem. I remarked to them that dialysis would no longer be needed anyway. They were not very pleased with my attitude, but again they said nothing to me about it. After all, my mental health was still being observed for normalcy. This attitude was certainly not normal.

The next day went by quickly. The doctors had still made no decision yet. I asked questions, but nobody was willing to let me know what was going on. The day for dialysis began very early in the morning with a visit from my kidney doctor. He was visibly upset and worried as he explained his situation to me again. He was waiting for more test results before he would make a decision. I took his hand and assured him that whatever decision he made would be the right one. I also let him know that I was not afraid and I had great faith in him. He left the room and told me that he would be back in a few minutes with his decision.

Those were the longest few minutes I can ever remember. It was a good thirty minutes. I held my rosary in my hands and began a prayer to the Blessed Mother to bless the doctors and staff in their decision. I had a positive outlook on the situation.

I began to doze off as I was praying, and at that moment the door to my room opened with great force. It startled me. My doctor bolted through the door and walked swiftly to my bed, waving my hospital chart in his hand and yelling, "Guess what!" I shouted back, "What?" My heart was pounding as he came to my bedside. He thrust the chart in front of me and exclaimed, "This is your chart. Your tests tell us that not only are your kidneys working again; they are filtering on their own. You no longer will need dialysis!" Soon, the nursing staff entered the room, and we hugged and cried. I looked my doctor in the eye and said, "See, I told you so!" I think at that moment they understood that something special had happened and there was no explanation for how or why it had happened. In the days to come, my special doctor shared his spirituality with me, and he told me about the respect that he had for my near-death experience. I will always remember that special doctor and the support that he gave me throughout my recovery.

The blood clot had dissolved on its own. In a couple of days, the shunt was removed from my arm. I was no longer dependent on a machine to stay alive.

After the Fact

As I was recuperating in the hospital, my recovery stunned the professionals who had tended to me: doctors, nurses, nurse aides, and technical support persons. Some of them had encouraged my family to remove me from life support, as my condition seemed so impossible to cure. There was no cure for what I had and my body was being physically attacked by my high fever and my convulsions. They were in awe of my quick recovery. They had no answers. I had a story to tell and they were eager to listen.

Two of the staff members told me that they had little faith in miracles, but after my recovery, their faith was strengthened. They had many stories to tell me about how their lives had been changed by caring for me.

The doctors asked me many questions to test my mental state. Staff members who were not related to my case would visit me and ask me questions. Many of their questions had to do with their spirituality. They told me about how the experience of my illness had strengthened their faith.

I endured many exams to test my physical and mental condition before they would let me leave the hospital. There were so many tests, and I was becoming so exhausted. After each test, the result was always positive. At one point, I felt like I could no longer endure another procedure, and I begged for them to stop. The neurologist had informed my family that when I was in crisis, the high fever and the condition that my body was in was destroying portions of my brain. The testing that was done on my brain before I was released from the hospital showed that these areas had healed and there was no sign of damage.

Finally, after fifty-nine days in the hospital, the time for my dismissal had come. It was a bittersweet departure, as I had come to love and appreciate all of the hospital team members who had taken such great care of me. I have saved the actual itemized bill of my stay at the hospital. I was admitted on May 15, 1973. I was discharged on July 13, 1973. The total amount of my bill was $19, 882.65. The portion of the bill that we had to pay was only $14. I can only guess how much that bill would add up to today.

The doctors could not believe that I was so healthy. I was dismissed from the hospital with only a bottle of special vitamins. No other medications were needed.

Finally, after many days and weeks, I was home! Life was a little hectic at first, but I soon became acquainted with schedules, meals, and school activities. I felt strong but I had been told to take it easy for a while. We had hired help with the housework and the children for some time until I could regain my strength.

Everything was so new to me because of my amnesia. I opened my closet and was amazed at all of my new clothes. Actually, I didn't remember them at first, but after a few days, memories began coming back to me. My greatest problem involved remembering people in my community. It was not hard for me to recognize people I had known for years. It was hard for me to identify people I had met within the previous five years or so. I would be shopping in a grocery store and someone would come up to me and give me a big hug. I had no idea who this person would be. This was embarrassing, to say the least. But when the word got out about my memory problem, friends were very patient. They helped me remember by telling me about special times that we had spent together. In a couple of weeks, my memory was completely restored, and I felt more comfortable about going out in public.

Approximately one year after I left the hospital, several nurses told me that on the last line of the last page of my hospital records, a doctor had written, " Whatever has happened in the recovery of this woman has not been in the hands of man. I term this a miracle."

The Sharing

Approximately one year after my illness, my friend Pat invited me to accompany her to Carmel Hall in Detroit. Carmel Hall was a housing and caring facility for senior citizens who needed assistance in their everyday living. Some of the residents also needed medical care, and there were also facilities for them at the hall. A very elegant and old hotel was converted into a beautiful residence for these seniors. My friend's aunt was a resident there, and we were going there to visit her.

As we entered the building, we proceeded to the dining room to have a quick cup of coffee and some nourishment. We opened the beautiful, thick, heavy glass doors and found a table, where we proceeded to sit down and enjoy our beverages. As I was glancing around the room, I observed an elderly gentleman sitting in a wheelchair eating his breakfast. For some reason, I could not keep my eyes off of him. He was of small stature, and he had long white hair and a long white beard. He reminded me of the picture of Moses in the Bible. I felt the urge to talk to him, but I did not want to interrupt his meal. I related this to my friend, and she was a bit short with me, reminding me that we had very little time and we needed to proceed to see her aunt.

As we left the area, I asked one of the Carmelite Sisters at the office what the gentleman's name was and if it was possible for me to see him later. She informed me that his name was Professor. This was the name the residents affectionately called him. He had been a popular and loving professor at a university in Detroit. She gave me his room number and advised me to visit him later.

I enjoyed this visit with my friend's aunt. I excused myself and told my friend that I was going to look for the professor before we had to leave. I told her that I would meet her in the dining room. As I approached the door to Professor's room, I could see that it was open. I knocked and nobody answered. I could tell that the room was empty. How disappointing this was to me. I questioned myself about the importance of the visit. I then glanced at the wall in his room as I was leaving the doorway. There on a wall was a beautiful crucifix. I had never seen such a cross before. Instead of the crucified Christ hanging from the cross, there was a resurrected Christ on the cross with his blessed arms outstretched toward me. How beautiful it was as it touched my spirit. I must have stood there for a couple of minutes just taking in the beauty. I then remembered that I had to meet my friend at the dining room before we began our journey back home to Owosso. I quickly proceeded to meet her.

As I approached the heavy glass doors into the dining room again, the professor was there, patiently waiting for someone to help him enter the room. I offered to help him through the doorway. After we had entered, I introduced myself and asked him for a few minutes of his time to visit with me. He was very cordial. We found a table and began our conversation. He introduced himself in his soft Spanish-English accent. I then asked him how he came to live at Carmel Hall.

It seems that he had been residing in an apartment at the university, where he still taught some classes and was a mentor to the students. One day he suffered a stroke in his room. He was unconscious for quite some time. By this time, I could hardly wait to hear where his story was going to take me. He then asked me if he could share with me the event that he had experienced while he was unconscious. Of course, I did not object and I asked him to continue.

He said that he had found himself in a very bright light, which surrounded him with a lot of love and peace. He likened this place to a place on a mountaintop where the air was very cool. He recalled that he remained there for a while, absorbed in the beauty of his surroundings. My heart began to beat a little faster as he continued. He then proceeded to explain how he had seen a small section of wall on the mountainside. There, he observed a printed message that was written in Spanish. It said, "My son, you are not to come yet, as I have work for you to do." He then told me that he remembers nothing else of that place and that event.

As a result of his stroke, he was physically unable to work at the university as a professor. He had come to Carmel Hall so that he could be assisted with his daily living. He became acquainted with the residents and staff, and he offered himself as a leader of the prayer community in the hall. He felt that by doing this he could serve the Lord in the best way that he knew how. He said that he felt very happy and fulfilled.

There was a short moment of complete silence. I then asked him if I could share my near-death experience with him. He was very interested in what I had to say, and he listened with great interest. When I was finished sharing my story with him, we just looked at each other with a mutually shared, profound understanding about what had happened to each of us. There were no words to express the feeling that we had between us. Here were two people who had been in the same wonderful place, and God had spoken to us with the same blessed message.

After this short silence, I asked him if I could correspond with him. He agreed. We shared addresses and said our goodbyes. Little did I know that we would never see each other again.

We corresponded for about a year. He would always send me wonderful and wise suggestions about how to live my life to the fullest. He would share with me his love for God. I looked forward to his letters coming in the mail. I also shared with him what was going on in my life, and he seemed so interested in those moments. He would always ask me about my family and how they were doing.

One day in October, I receive a phone call from the sisters at Carmel Hall. My beloved Professor had died. I then prepared for my journey to say goodbye to my dear friend. I arrived at the hall, and the sisters were most gracious. They invited me to stay with them. We drove to the funeral home, where Professor was being shown. As I approached the casket, I could see how perfectly peaceful he looked. The expression on his face was one of peace and happiness. In my heart, I knew that he was home. Finally, he could see the face of the God, which had spoken to him on that mountaintop. Perhaps the Lord was thanking him for a job well done.

The funeral was beautifully simple and holy. After the funeral, the sisters approached me with a wrapped gift in their hands. They informed me that the professor had wanted me to have one of his possessions. I opened the gift and there was the cross of the resurrected

Christ that had been hanging on his wall. With great honor, the cross hung in our home. Looking at that cross, I would think about this very special person who had touched my heart in a most blessed way.

Conclusion

Before having this wonderful experience, I was not sure what my purpose on earth was. It was a nagging question in my mind. I knew that I had so much to live for, but I needed to have this question answered.

After learning from God in His light, I now understood that the answer was very simple. The purpose of our living is to serve God. Ask Him to show you how and He will open the doors for you.

The years following my illness were very busy. Four young children had turned into teenagers. They had very active lives, and I found myself busier than ever. I volunteered in several organizations. Life was hectic but good. I kept looking for God to open that special door for me.

In 1981, there was an article in the local newspaper that informed the public that a hospice was being formed in our area and applications for volunteers were available. Hospice is a special concept of care that is provided to patients and families who face a terminal illness. Volunteers are part of a hospice team that cares for the family. I instantly knew that this was what I wanted to do. I wanted to be a volunteer who served those who were dying. I wanted to help people transition to the next world in a peaceful and meaningful manner. I took the classes and soon found myself helping in the hospice office. I helped train the volunteers by typing lessons and just being in class to help the instructor. It wasn't long before I was qualified to become a volunteer coordinator. I also was a volunteer, and I was assigned to hospice families. In my heart, I had found what I loved to do. It was the answer to how I was to serve the Lord.

Today, I still have the honor of being a hospice volunteer. I find a lot of satisfaction in serving hospice patients and their families. It is my privilege to be with a person as they are dying. It is an honor to serve the family whose loved one is dying.

I put my heart and soul into my hospice work. My career in hospice work would be the subject for another book. It has been the most fulfilling career I could have ever imagined. I have truly received the most blessings serving hospice patients. I worked with the hospice office for seventeen years. I am still a proud hospice volunteer today.

Throughout this experience, I have obtained much knowledge about living and dying. My life has changed for the better. I know that when we die we have a choice to be with God. I know that when we live, we are supposed to serve God and His children. I know that we are supposed to be strong and firm in our spiritual convictions. I know that we are supposed to pray for others who are dying so that they might be strong in their faith.

Our four beautiful children have grown and left home, and they have established lives of their own. We have six beautiful grandchildren. My husband and I are enjoying our retirement. We are very busy volunteering in our community, and we stay involved in our church. We spend time relaxing and doing what we want to do in God's great land.

We have been through many difficulties throughout the years following my illness, but our love for each other has made us strong.

We have come to appreciate every year that we have with each other. Something that could have been a great tragedy in our lives turned out to be a blessing. We shall always remember this, and we will always be eternally grateful for God's great blessings.

One lesson that I have learned in life is that no matter what trials you might go through, when it is over, look for the lesson that it has brought you. It might not be instantaneous, but with patience and trust in the Lord, He will show you this lesson. He will show you that it was He who was with you all of the time.

Do not fear death because life continues on afterward in a much better place. We miss those who go before us, but know that they are in the arms of the Lord and they will always be with you in spirit.

Death is a bridge to a glorious life—a life that is free from pain and suffering. This life will let you see the face of God and be enveloped in His light of love and peace.

I have had a long and exciting life. There is not one emotion or feeling that I have not experienced. I have not traveled all over the world, but I have had the experience of leaving this world briefly. The memory of this experience will be with me forever.

May God richly bless you and those you love.

Maureen

Poem

This is a poem that my sister-in-law Lynn Bishop wrote in 1992. She handed me a hand-written copy of it shortly after she wrote it.

I rediscovered this poem shortly after I finished this manuscript. She has given me permission to print this in my book. I think it is a very comforting poem. Thank you, Lynn.

Birth Light

Set free your spirit, move toward the light,

For all that is here on earth is night.

Lift up your heart, release your soul to me,

The death of body sets us free.

For surely this is hell and heaven's light

Entices us to leave this night.

Freedom of the spirit is but birth

To something else besides this earth.

My heart is ever with you till the day

It is your turn to light my way.

It is through pain of birth that we are here.

This too is birth, though much less clear.

Move toward the light and do not be afraid.

Tis through your death, your birth is made.

Poem printed with permission from Lynn Todd Bishop.

Written in memory of her brother, Lee Girard,
September 21, 1991.